MW00675025

HISTORY & GEOGRAPHY 707
Economics—Resources and Need

LIFEPAC Test is located in the center of the booklet. Please remove before starting the unit.

Author:
Alpha Omega Staff

Editor:
Alan Christopherson, M.S.

Westover Studios Design Team:
Phillip Pettet, Creative Lead
Teresa Davis, DTP Lead
Nick Castro
Andi Graham
Jerry Wingo

Alpha Omega
PUBLICATIONS

804 N. 2nd Ave. E.
Rock Rapids, IA 51246-1759

Economics—Resources and Need

Introduction

Economics is the study of the consumption, production, and distribution of wealth. It deals with our wants as human beings, the resources we possess, and the choices we have to make. Economists use a variety of methods and tools in their work. They are interested in the market, competition, government, and money. In this LIFEPAC® you will see how these tools apply to our economic system. You will read what the Bible says about economics, and you will also start to develop a personal financial program.

Objectives

Read these objectives. The objectives tell you what you will be able to do when you have successfully completed this LIFEPAC. When you have finished this LIFEPAC, you should be able to:

1. Define economics.

2. Differentiate wants from needs.

3. Describe supply and demand.

4. Describe how prices regulate supply and demand.

5. Describe savings and investments.

6. Explain the difference between a producer's and a consumer's market.

7. Make a comparison between free enterprise and communism.

8. Describe the function of taxes.

9. Describe how government can regulate the economy.

10. Describe the characteristics and functions of money.

11. Develop a sound personal financial program.

12. Make wiser choices as a consumer.

13. Tell what the Bible says about money management.

Survey the LIFEPAC. Ask yourself some questions about this study and write your questions here.

1. WHAT IS ECONOMICS?

Economics is the study of the production, distribution, and consumption of wealth. A direct relationship exists between the things wanted or needed, and the resources that are available.

In this first section you will learn about this relationship and how you, as a consumer, can make wise choices.

SECTION OBJECTIVES

Review these objectives. When you have completed this section, you should be able to:

1. Define economics.
2. Differentiate wants from needs.
3. Describe supply and demand.
12. Make wiser choices as a consumer.

VOCABULARY

Study these words to enhance your learning success in this section.

agrarian (u grãr′ ē un). Having to do with farming, using, or owning land; agricultural.

consumers (kun sü′ murz). People whose wants are satisfied.

communism (ko′ mü ni zum). Economic system in which the government controls all economic decisions.

economics (ek u nom′ iks). The study of the production, distribution, and consumption of wealth.

economic system (ek u nom′ ik sis′ tum). Organized system by which a nation uses its resources to satisfy its wants.

free enterprise (frē en′ tur prīz). Economic system of the United States.

market (mar′ ket). Demand for commodity or service.

producers (pro dü′ surz). Human resources.

subsidy (sub′ su dē). Money granted by the government.

Note: *All vocabulary words in this LIFEPAC appear in* **boldface** *print the first time they are used. If you are not sure of the meaning when you are reading, study the definitions given.*

Pronunciation Key: hat, āge, cãre, fär; let, ēqual, tėrm; it, īce; hot, ōpen, ôrder; oil; out; cup, pút, rüle; child; long; thin; /ŦH/ for then; /zh/ for measure; /u/ or /ə/ represents /a/ in about, /e/ in taken, /i/ in pencil, /o/ in lemon, and /u/ in circus.

HUMAN WANTS

Since **economics** studies the production, distribution, and consumption of wealth, it is concerned with human wants and needs. Each country or society has a great variety of wants and needs. Wherever they live, people always seem to want more food, clothes, houses, cars, recreation, and services. Such normal human wants are limitless. A list of all our wants would probably be quite lengthy. However, care must be taken not to confuse our wants with our needs. The Bible says in Matthew 6:31 through 33 that we should not worry about having an abundance to eat or to wear. Our heavenly Father knows that we need food and clothing. He will give them to us if we seek His kingdom and His righteousness. Wants, then, are limitless and varied, but food, clothing, and shelter are the basic needs.

Simple societies. In the United States human wants and needs are very different from those of other countries. United States citizens have been blessed with food, clothing, automobiles, and lovely homes. Even the poorest people in this country earn more money than three-fourths of the rest of the people in the world. In the underdeveloped nations of Africa, Asia, and Latin America, the people barely have enough to eat. What people in the United States earn in a month is often more than others in the world earn in a year. Many of these poor people live on one scant meal a day, but we usually have three meals in addition to some snacks.

Thousands of people around the world live in crowded, crude homes. Often they have no sanitary facilities and no water. They sleep on mats or bare floors, and their clothing is sparse. For these people, life is a struggle to fulfill the needs for survival.

Most people in the underdeveloped countries are farmers, but few have tools or machines to help work their land efficiently. The little money they earn is spent on keeping themselves and their families alive. Nearly every penny is taken just to do that. They have no money to invest in machinery, factories, roads, and schools. The people, by and large, are uneducated. Without education they do not have the skills and knowledge to use the resources of their land. This lack of skills and knowledge creates a vicious cycle of more poverty and less education.

As was mentioned before, most of the people living in underdeveloped countries are farmers. Therefore, they have a fairly simple society. Each person depends first on themself and on their immediate family to supply their needs from the land. If the persons needs cannot be supplied that way, they then turn to relatives and neighbors for trade and assistance. When this source fails, the family will probably starve. Where else could they turn? Without money they are unable to buy food and clothing or even the seed to plant their crops. The governments do not have the money to carry out complete **subsidy** programs.

Complex societies. In this country, however, a much more complex society exists. Some people may grow a few vegetables or even some meat; but on the whole, we are all very dependent upon others for our needs. Huge farms and ranches grow our fruits, vegetables, and meats. Besides the farmers, we rely on the companies who process the food in cans, bottles, or packages. We rely on the people who transport the goods to the stores. Beyond that, we rely on the storekeepers to keep things in stock for us. If any part of this chain breaks down, we are virtually helpless to take care of our basic human needs. If truck drivers go on strike and refuse to bring us meat and dairy products, we have to go without. Even though we are a rich country, we are very dependent upon other people to satisfy our needs.

This dependence includes people from other countries. Since we are such a wealthy land, we can afford goods and services from around the

| Complex Society

world. Other nations produce the cars, electronic equipment, cameras, watches, and toys that we want. If our relations with those countries break down, we can no longer depend on the supply of these imported products.

Other societies. Between our very complex society and the very simple societies of the underdeveloped countries are the societies that are a combination of the two extremes. Countries with such societies are basically **agrarian**, or farming, but also have some of the characteristics of a more complex society. The people farm the land, but they use machinery and are educated in how to raise the best crops and how to use their resources efficiently. They can make a profit on their crops and other goods.

That profit enables them to buy different goods and services and to raise their standard of living. These people are not dependent only upon their own families and relatives as the people of simple societies are. They also are not totally dependent upon other countries as complex societies are. They are balanced between the two types of economy.

Complete these statements.

1.1 Human wants are _____ .

1.2 The _____ says that we should not worry about having an abundance to eat and wear.

1.3 Boats, games, and chocolate are a partial list of human _____ .

1.4 Our _____ are the basics of food, clothing, and shelter.

1.5 A society in which a person depends primarily on themself and his family to supply theri needs from the land is called a _____ society.

Match the following.

1.6 _____ economic system

1.7 _____ complex society

1.8 _____ economics

1.9 _____ free enterprise

1.10 _____ communism

1.11 _____ cars

1.12 _____ market

1.13 _____ producers

1.14 _____ agrarian

1.15 _____ consumers

1.16 _____ subsidy

1.17 _____ simple societies

a. a want
b. organized system by which a nation use its resources to satisfy its wants
c. underdeveloped countries
d. relies on many people, corporations, and countries to supply the needs of people
e. money granted by the government
f. the study of the production, distribution, and consumption of wealth
g. people whose wants are satisfied
h. economic system of the United States
i. having to do with farming, using, or owning land; agricultural
j. economic system in which the government controls all economic decisions
k. human resources
l. demand for commodity or service

ECONOMIC SYSTEMS

An **economic system** is a way of satisfying people's wants. Since people's wants vary according to the type of society, more than one economic system exists in the world. Two major economic systems today are **free enterprise** and socialism.

Free enterprise. Our economic system is called *free enterprise*. All businesses are privately owned. Prices and the availability of all goods and services are determined by the forces of supply and demand. As people want or demand something, business makes it available. The price is decided by how badly people want the product and by how many of the items business makes available. In free enterprise, government does not interfere in this process known as the free **market**.

No country has a pure free enterprise system, but countries with a small amount of government control over business, are said to have a free enterprise system.

Even though problems with inflation and high prices exist in this country, the United States is still fortunate in having an extremely high standard of living and almost complete economic freedom. We are truly blessed by God and have much to be thankful for. Millions of people in other countries would consider luxuries the things that are considered "needs" here. Pause for just a moment and thank God for all the things with which He has blessed you.

Socialism. Another economic system is called socialism. In this kind of system, the government is very much involved. Although less rigid than **communism**, which exercises almost complete government control, socialism has more government control than the free enterprise system. The government often owns things, such as railroads and the coal and steel industries. Some of the industries are owned by private citizens, and supply and demand helps to control the prices. The people are allowed to protest against economic policies and government control when they have a democratic form of government. In general, however, they do not have the economic freedom known in the United States. Some of the countries that are partly socialist are Great Britain, India, and Sweden.

 Answer true or false.

1.18 _____ The economic system in the United States is called *free enterprise*.

1.19 _____ Under communism prices are determined by supply and demand.

1.20 _____ A considerable amount of government control is found in the socialist system.

1.21 _____ Communism is a system in which the government controls almost all economic activity.

RESOURCES AVAILABLE

Think about the things that you would like to have, such as a bicycle, a skateboard, clothes, books, tapes, or CDs. These items are your human wants. When you receive your allowance or money that you have earned, you may look at it and feel rich for awhile, until you realize that it can only be exchanged for a small fraction of your wants. Your allowance represents your available resources. One of the basic problems in economics is that human wants are limitless, but resources are not. However hard society works, it will never be able to keep up with all the wants of the people, just as your income will never be able to supply all of your wants, until you learn the truth of Matthew 6:33 and Luke 12:15b.

The limitless wants have to be satisfied by the available resources, both human and nonhuman. When the United States was first being settled, the people thought that limitless amounts of fuel, timber, water, animals, land, minerals, and clean air were available. Now, however, we realize that these resources have been overused and in many cases, severely depleted. The wants of some people were satisfied without consideration for the needs of others. One of the things that economists today are trying to do is to restore a balance between the resources people are using up and the resources we still possess.

As our country progressed into the Industrial Revolution, it began using other kinds of resources—labor (people) and machinery. Even these resources have not been able to supply all of our human wants. Do not forget that all our resources are limited and, in many cases, are scarce when compared to human wants. To get more of one product or service, we may have to become willing to be satisfied with less of another.

Wants can be satisfied in different ways and resources can also be used in a variety of ways. Remembering your available resources (your allowance or earned money), consider your list of wants again. Instead of buying a new bicycle or skateboard, why not buy a used one–or at least wait until they go on sale? The money you save could be spent on other things. Some stores even sell used books, tapes, and CDs. Have you looked for these stores? Part of using resources wisely is intelligently investigating the many possible alternatives.

| Our unlimited wants have to be satisfied by limited resources.

 **Write the letter of the correct answer on each line.**

1.22 Limitless wants have to be satisfied by _____ .
    a. available resources   b. government   c. parents

1.23 Two new kinds of resources developed in the Industrial Revolution were _____ .
    a. water and wind   b. people and machines   c. sugar and wool

1.24 Bicycles and skateboards are _____ .
    a. needs   b. wants   c. resources

1.25 Early settlers thought many resources like land, fuel, and water were _____ .
    a. important to conserve   b. limited   c. limitless

CHOICE

Our wants are limitless, but our available resources are not. This fact leads us to the basic problem in economics. The problem is one of distributing the available resources to best satisfy human wants. Choice is the deciding factor. As we have seen, each nation has an organized economic system by which it uses its resources to satisfy its wants. This system provides a method for making decisions. As you recall, the system used in the United States is called free enterprise, the system in which private businesses operate with little government regulation. The other major economic system is called socialism, the system in which private businesses operate with more government regulation than free enterprise, and in which the government may own some businesses. The countries of the world use either free enterprise, socialism, or a combination of the two.

The labor force. Problems in production and distribution can develop within the free enterprise system, however. One of these problems is the organization of the labor force. Unemployed people will always exist, to a greater or lesser extent; and many jobs, such as repairing streets, designing aircraft, or improving homes of poor people, need to be done. Getting the people working at the jobs that need to be done is difficult. The problem lies in matching the importance of the job to be done with the wage to be paid the worker. The **consumer** indirectly decides on the need and value of a job by deciding to pay for a product or service.

In our country a diversity of human wants must be satisfied. People want cars, houses, boats, sports equipment, and many other things. Many people working together are needed to produce any one of these items. To manufacture a car takes materials like steel, rubber, cloth, and plastics. When these materials are formed the car must be assembled. A great deal of planning and many jobs are involved in this one item. The economic importance of these cars, however, depends on the number manufactured. The country can have too many cars, or perhaps not enough. A problem exists in getting the right things produced by the right people in the right amounts.

Even after the right goods have been produced, they must be distributed. The cars, food, sports equipment, or toys will not be used if they never leave the factory. This distribution brings many more people into the picture. The efficiency of these people also is important to the country as a whole. Again we see that complex societies are very dependent on others for their well-being.

Complete the following statements.

1.26 The basic problem in economics is distributing the available resources to best satisfy human

_____ .

1.27 The economic system of the United States is called _____ .

1.28 People in _____ societies are dependent upon others for their well-being.

1.29 After goods have been produced, they must be _____ to the market place where they can be sold to consumers.

Decisions. Our economic system helps us to make four basic decisions:

1. *What* goods and services should be produced,

2. *How* goods and services should be produced,

3. *Who* should have the goods and services produced, and

4. *How* much of these goods and services should be produced.

Many of these decisions are made by the consumer. Consumers are the people whose wants are satisfied. Every human being is a consumer. Some of the things we consume are used up quickly—ice cream, meat, concert tickets; others are used over longer time periods—houses, cars, clothes, appliances, and so forth. Services that are performed for us by others are also considered as consumed goods—haircuts, dry cleaning, and auto repairs. **Producers** are the human resources that make the products or perform the services.

How do we know what goods and services to produce? Consumers determine what will be produced by deciding what they are willing to spend their money on. Business people make things that they think people will buy. They are trying to make a profit and will often try to

influence the consumer with advertising and other selling activities.

How should goods and services be produced? To a business person, profit is often the main factor in making this decision. They have to decide how to produce their goods in the cheapest manner to make the most profit. Sometimes the best decision, for example, would be to use simple tools and a large amount of labor. At other times, however, using machines and just a small amount of labor might be better. The businessperson also has to take into account how efficient their employees are, how much the rent is for their land and buildings, how many jobs are available, the risks involved, and so on.

Who should have the goods and services produced? The incomes of the consumers usually determine this decision. The people who make larger incomes are naturally able to acquire larger amounts of the things produced. This factor especially affects the production of "luxury" items.

How much of the different goods and services should be produced? This decision is determined by the demand for the product. As long as a company can sell its goods for a profit, it will continue to produce more. In other words, as the demand for a product increases, the supply will also be increased by the producer.

Complete the following activity.

1.30 What four basic decisions does our economic system help us make?

a. _____

b. _____

c. _____

d. _____

Match the word with the best definition.

1.31 _____ consumers

1.32 _____ businessmen

1.33 _____ income

1.34 _____ demand

1.35 _____ producers

a. decide how to produce goods to make a profit

b. determines how much will be produced

c. decide what to produce by what they are willing to buy

d. the human resources that make products or perform the services

e. determines who will get what is produced

Complete this activity.

1.36 Use your school library, your local library, or the internet to find some information about an underdeveloped country, such as Haiti, Nicaragua, Bangladesh, or Cambodia. Find out what is grown or mined in that country. Are the products imported into this country? When you have completed this work discuss your findings in groups and write down your information to share with the class.

TEACHER CHECK _____ _____
                    initials   date

 **Answer this question.**

1.37 What kind of economic system does the underdeveloped country studied in Activity 1.36 have?

_____

TEACHER CHECK _____ _____
                                                initials   date

Review the material in this section in preparation for the Self Test. The Self Test will check your mastery of this particular section. The items missed on this Self Test will indicate specific areas where restudy is needed for mastery.

SELF TEST 1

Write the correct letter on each line (each answer, 2 points).

1.01 Who influences the decision of what to produce because of their willingness to buy? _____
    a. consumer   b. producer   c. business person   d. agrarian

1.02 Every human being is a _____ .
    a. consumer   b. producer   c. business person   d. agrarian

1.03 What requires a large income? _____
    a. consumer   b. agrarian   c. business person
    d. luxury items   e. subsidy

1.04 Human resources that make products are called _____ .
    a. consumers   b. producers   c. business people
    d. luxury items   e. agrarians

1.05 The deciding factor in allocating resources is _____ .
    a. the consumer   b. producer   c. business person
    d. choice   e. unemployment

1.06 Who or what decides how goods and services should be produced? _____
    a. producer   b. business person   c. luxury items   d. unemployment

1.07 What word means *having to do with farming*? _____
a. consumer b. business person c. producer d. agrarian

1.08 What will always exist in any economic system? _____
a. luxury items b. subsidy c. choice d. unemployment

1.09 Who tries to make a profit and influence customers? _____
a. consumer b. producer c. business person

1.010 Money granted by the government is called _____ .
a. welfare b. producer money c. a subsidy d. consumer money

Answer true or false (each answer, 1 point).

1.011 _____ Human wants are limitless.

1.012 _____ Available resources are limitless.

1.013 _____ Our resources can only supply a small fraction of our wants.

1.014 _____ The early settlers thought that the land, timber, animals and water resources were limited.

Complete the following statements (each answer, 3 points).

1.015 Our economic system in the United States is called _____ .

1.016 The people whose needs and wants are satisfied are called _____ .

1.017 Services that are performed for us are considered to be *consumed* _____ .

1.018 The study of consumption, production, and distribution of wealth is called

_____ .

1.019 God has promised to supply our _____ .

1.020 In general, the wants of the people are greater than their available _____ .

1.021 Human wants _____ be completely satisfied.

1.022 The organized way by which a nation uses its resources to satisfy its wants is called its

_____ system.

1.023 Businesses have to produce goods in the cheapest manner to make the most _____ .

Write the correct letter on each line (each answer, 2 points).

1.024 If a product is in great demand, the producer will supply _____ .
a. more   b. less   c. the same

1.025 Limitless wants have to be satisfied by _____ .
a. consumers   b. available resources
c. economic systems

1.026 Human wants do not include _____ .
a. a new car   b. a place to live
c. books   d. a mansion with a swimming pool

1.027 Needs do not include _____ .
a. a new boat   b. food   c. clothing

1.028 Society will never be able to keep up with _____ .
a. the available resources   b. the wants of the people
c. businesses

Answer these questions (each numbered item, 5 points).

1.029 What four basic decisions does our economic system help us make?

a. _____

b. _____

c. _____

d. _____

1.030 What is the meaning of *economics*?

_____

_____

Complete the following statements (each numbered item, 3 points).

1.031 The economic system in which consumers control prices and production through supply and demand is called _____ .

1.032 The economic system in which the government is in almost complete control of economic activity is _____ .

1.033 If the demand for a product increases, the _____ will also increase.

1.034 The economic system that has a moderate amount of governmental control is called _____ .

66/83 SCORE_____ TEACHER_____ _____
initials   date

2. METHODS AND TOOLS OF THE ECONOMIST

You have learned what economics is about and understand wants, needs, and resources. You also have studied something about the decisions involved in production and consumption.

In this section you will study the market mechanism and how competition, government, and money affect it.

SECTION OBJECTIVES

Review these objectives. When you have completed this section, you should be able to:

4. Describe how prices regulate supply and demand.

5. Describe savings and investments.

6. Explain the difference between a producer's and a consumer's market.

7. Make a comparison between free enterprise and communism.

8. Describe the function of taxes.

9. Describe how government can regulate the economy.

10. Describe the characteristics and functions of money.

12. Make wiser choices as a consumer.

VOCABULARY

Study these words to enhance your learning success in this section.

capital (cap' u tul). Man-made resources used in the production of other goods.

competition (com pu ti' shun). Economic rivalry among sellers for the consumer's dollars.

consumer's market (cun sü' murz mar' kut). Lower prices for consumers because of much competition between producers.

entrepreneur (än' tru pru nėr'). Businessman who takes on and guides an enterprise.

investment (in vest' munt). Spending on capital goods.

money (mun' ē). Bank deposits; the demand deposits on which people write checks.

monopoly (mu nop' u lē). Complete control of trade in a commodity.

producer's market (pru dü' surz mär' kut). Producers are not satisfying consumer's wants and are making large profits.

saving (sāv' ing). Abstaining from consumption; not using.

MARKET MECHANISM

In the previous section you learned that wants for goods and services are satisfied by the combined use of available resources. The combined resources are the factors of production and include land or natural resources, labor or human resources, capital goods or man-made resources, and **entrepreneurs**.

Natural resources are those materials found in nature which man puts to his use. Minerals, trees, animals, and water are all used as raw materials for the things man produces and consumes.

Human resources are all the people in society who work and, by working, become producers. The quality of education or training that these people receive is an important factor in both the production and the quality of their goods and services.

Capital goods are man-made resources that are used in the production of other goods. These resources include such things as factories, buildings, machines, computers, and so on.

Entrepreneurs are business people who manage production. They raise the money to start a business and to keep it going. They also decide what resources the business will use, and they organize the people who will run the business.

How the consumer spends money determines what is produced. If the consumer will not buy a product, no reason exists for anyone to produce it. Production is also affected by the amount of profit that can be made. The entrepreneurs will usually choose the means of production that will assure them the largest profit while still maintaining enough quality to attract buyers. They realize that they need to use their resources efficiently to produce a good product that will earn them a large profit.

How much is to be produced is directly related to the demand for the item or service. As the total demand for something increases or decreases, total production also will increase or decrease respectively.

In the market mechanism of the United States, producers have discovered that division of labor and specialization have done much to close the gap between our unlimited wants and our limited resources.

 Complete the following statements.

2.1 Natural resources are _____

_____ .

2.2 Capital goods are _____ that are used in

the production of other goods.

2.3 Entrepreneurs are _____ who take on and guide an enterprise.

2.4 Human resources are the people in the society who are _____ .

Match these vocabulary words with their definitions.

2.5 _____ capital

2.6 _____ competition

2.7 _____ consumer's market

2.8 _____ investment

2.9 _____ money

2.10 _____ monopoly

2.11 _____ producer's market

2.12 _____ saving

a. abstaining from consumption; not using

b. man-made resources used in the production of other goods

c. producers are not satisfying consumer's wants and are making large profits

d. economic rivalry among sellers for the consumer's dollars

e. complete control of trade in a commodity

f. lower prices for consumers because of much competition between producers

g. the demand deposits on which people write checks

h. spending on capital goods

Division of labor. Division of labor means that one person does a small portion of work on a bigger project. At a later time, all the small parts are joined together to form the finished product. This procedure has proved to be a very efficient way to mass produce items.

One of the industries that uses this system to good advantage is the auto industry. In fact, Henry Ford first utilized mass production. If each employee in an automobile factory had to build an entire car by himself, it would take a very long time, and the cars would be very

| Mass Production

expensive. If the employees divide up the work, however, the work goes much more quickly and keeps the cost down. Although the person who builds a car from start to finish by himself might do a better job and might be more exacting, the cost would be so high that very few people could afford a car. Since Americans want many cars in a variety of sizes and styles and in a price range that is affordable, the auto industry uses mass production to try to satisfy wants. This mass production is an example of the market mechanism at work. The consumers determine how many goods are produced and, indirectly, the manner in which they are produced.

Specialization. Specialization is much the same as division of labor. Individuals, businesses, and different geographical regions specialize in producing certain products. With specialization, more work can be done more efficiently. An architect can design good buildings. A construction company, including plumbers and electricians, can erect them. The finished products are better and more economical because the workers do that part of the job that they are best trained to do. A region or a country will produce the things that use the most abundant and, therefore, the cheapest resources. Specialization enables more goods to be produced. It also causes a greater need for trade.

Wisconsin is famous for its cheese, and it produces more than the people of that state can consume. Arizona has an abundance of citrus. Therefore, Wisconsin sends its cheese to Arizona, and Arizona sends its citrus to Wisconsin. As a consequence of their specialization, these two regions become interdependent. This same thing happens between individuals and between countries. All of us depend on many other people to provide us with wanted goods and services.

| Wisconsin's cheese industry is an example of specialization.

The businesses that manufacture or distribute products provide the incomes of their workers. Businesses also provide income by the rental of land and buildings and through buying raw materials from other businessmen. These incomes then enable more people to become consumers and begin the cycle of unlimited consumer wants all over again.

The market mechanism is the basis for our whole American economy. It provides the means for consumers to make decisions. Through the market the consumers and producers, the savers and investors, decide what goods and services will be produced, how they will be produced, and who will get them. The market mechanism is the only tangible way our demands can be expressed to producers. In return, the producers can respond to consumers by using their resources to produce the things we most desire. Each consumer plays an important role in the economy by the decisions they make.

HISTORY & GEOGRAPHY 707

LIFEPAC TEST

NAME _____

DATE _____

SCORE _____

60
___
75

HISTORY & GEOGRAPHY 707: LIFEPAC TEST

Match these items (each answer, 2 points).

1. _____ wants
2. _____ supply
3. _____ economics
4. _____ needs
5. _____ saving
6. _____ demand
7. _____ price
8. _____ taxes
9. _____ investment
10. _____ entrepreneur
11. _____ producer
12. _____ consumers

a. businessman

b. abstaining from consumption; not using

c. people whose wants are satisfied

d. what people want to have produced

e. amount of a good produced

f. study of production, consumption, and distribution of wealth

g. human resource

h. collected by government to provide public services

i. desires

j. amount charged for goods and services

k. basics of life; food, clothing, shelter

l. spending on capital goods

Match the following (each answer, 2 points).

13. _____ consumer's market

14. _____ communism

15. _____ financial program

16. _____ choice

17. _____ producer's market

18. _____ free enterprise

19. _____ government

20. _____ reserves

21. _____ economic system

22. _____ competition

23. _____ capital goods

24. _____ factors of production

25. _____ money

a. regulates economic system, collects taxes, balances total supply and demand

b. bank deposits; demand deposits on which people write checks

c. competition between producers and low prices for consumers

d. land, labor, capital goods, entrepreneurship

e. economic system in which the government controls economic decisions

f. man-made resources used in production

g. includes budget and wise use of money

h. economic rivalry among sellers

i. problems of distributing resources to best satisfy wants

j. organized means by which a nation uses its resources to satisfy its wants

k. producers are under-supplying and making a large profit

l. gold which backs up currency

m. economic system of the United States

Write the letter for the correct answer on each line (each answer, 2 points).

26.   Human wants must be satisfied by _____ .
a. consumers   b. available resources
c. economic systems

27.   Society as a whole can never keep up with _____ .
a. entrepreneurs   b. available resources
c. the wants of the people

28.   Specialization causes people, regions, and countries to become more _____ .
a. interdependent   b. independent   c. communistic

29.   When the supply of a product is less than the demand, prices and profits _____ .
a. rise   b. fall   c. remain the same

30.   Taxes the government collects are spent on _____ .
a. natural resources   b. public goods and services
c. market mechanism

31.   Which of the following does the Bible advise for economic success? _____
a. debt   b. hasty decisions   c. hard work

32.   Which of the following is not a function of money? _____
a. acts as a medium of exchange   b. serves as store of value
c. gives a measure of value   d. provides a source of contentment

33.   Which of the following is created by mass production? _____
a. custom made jewelry   b. novels
c. computers   d. balancing supply and demand

34.   The borrower is _____ .
a. important to the lender   b. happier to the lender
c. servant to the lender

35.   A tithe means _____ .
a. a gift   b. 10 per cent   c. a Biblical message

Answer the following question (this question worth a total of 5 points).

36.   Our economic system helps us make four important decisions. What are they?

a. _____

b. _____

c. _____

d. _____

Answer true or false.

2.13 _____ Division of labor means one person does a small portion of a larger project.

2.14 _____ As demand increases, production decreases.

2.15 _____ Consumers determine how much is produced.

2.16 _____ Specialization is very different from division of labor.

Prices. Prices keep the businesses producing what the consumer wants to buy and paying out incomes to people for producing goods and services. When the demand for something is greater than the available supply, prices and profits generally rise. Then production is increased and the supply and demand become more equal. In the opposite way, when the supply of something is greater than the demand for it, prices generally fall. Since that also makes profits fall, the producers tend to move into other kinds of production that will make them more profit.

Savings and investments. For any economy to remain stable or to expand, **savings** and **investments** are necessary. Savings means abstaining from or at least postponing consumption. **Money** is saved rather than spent for the goods and services wanted. This money is put in the bank, savings and loan association, or credit union, where it can be loaned to entrepreneurs.

In economics, investment means spending money on capital goods. The more a country invests in making capital goods such as factories and machines, the more it can produce. Another important investment for society is education. It improves the quality of labor and it increases productivity.

Education leads to technological progress. Technology makes possible the development of complicated machinery for mass production of goods, for synthetics (nylon, plastic, detergent), and for substitutes (plastic, plywood, particle board). Research has also helped apply science to agriculture so that pests are better controlled and crops give a greater yield. All these developments have helped teach us how to use our natural resources carefully and efficiently.

Complete the following sentences.

2.17 Savings means _____ .

2.18 Investment means spending money on _____ .

Discuss in class.

2.19 How is your education an investment in society?

_____

_____

Match these items.

2.20 _____ savings

2.21 _____ investments

2.22 _____ prices rise

2.23 _____ prices fall

2.24 _____ education

a. leads to technological progress

b. demand greater than supply

c. spending money on capital goods

d. abstaining from consumption

e. supply greater than demand

COMPETITION

One essential part of our market mechanism is **competition**. Competition is economic rivalry among sellers for the consumer's dollars.

An example of competition at work is price competition. If several sellers are competing for the consumer's dollars, the price of the product will go down to the lowest level possible that will still cover the cost of production and provide a reasonable profit. The businesses that are making efficient use of their resources will be able to survive. The ones that cannot attract enough of the consumers' money to meet their costs and make some profit, will be forced to stop production.

Competition also exists in an area not directly involved with prices. This competition includes such things as improvement of the product, improvement in the way it is presented to the public—the packaging, the variety of sizes—or improvement in the advertising of the product.

Consumer's market. Our market system is often called a **consumer's market** or a **producer's market**, depending on the effects of competition at the time. In the consumer's market, competition among producers is keen and helps to keep them using their prices to attract more customers. They are also forcing producers out of the market who are not using their resources efficiently or are not producing things wanted by the consumer. Because of this practice, the consumer reaps the benefits. The market, therefore, is a consumer's market.

Producer's market. In a producer's market goods are not being produced at the rate of demand. Because of this, producers can ask for high prices that will give them large profits. In this market producers do not need to be as efficient as they must be in a consumer's market. Consumers will pay high prices because the goods are in short supply and competition between the buyers is lacking.

 Answer true or false.

2.25 _____ One essential of the market mechanism is competition.

2.26 _____ Competition means that no rivalry exists among sellers.

2.27 _____ A consumer's market means that competition among sellers is poor.

2.28 _____ A producer's market means higher prices.

2.29 _____ A consumer's market means lower prices.

Circle the answers that complete the statement.

2.30 In a consumer's market:

prices for consumers rise.

competition is keen.

producers must use resources efficiently.

products must be improved.

2.31 In a producer's market:

producers do not have to use resources efficiently.

producers make large profits.

prices for consumers drop.

consumers' wants cannot be satisfied.

Complete this activity.

2.32 First, ask your teacher to arrange for this activity with a local store owner. Then ask the store-keeper for some information about a specific item they sell. Find out whether its price has changed in the past year. Find out what the demand is for that item. If the price of the item is reduced for a sale, do more of the items sell? Write your information down on your own paper.

TEACHER CHECK _____ _____
                                    initials   date

Complete the following statement.

2.33 _____ is *rivalry among sellers for consumer's dollars.*

Free Enterprise

Communism

Free enterprise vs. communism. The economic system of many countries, including the United States, is called free enterprise. The owners of business and industry are called capitalists. The government intervenes in certain economic matters, but generally the consumers and producers make the economic decisions.

Communism, however, is a different system. Communists believe that the capitalists exploit the workers and do not give them what they deserve in return for their work. They think that the means of production should belong to the people as a whole. They want no owners to exploit the workers. In a communist country the state, or nation, owns all of the natural resources, all industry, power plants, railroads, airlines and ships, banks, television and radio networks, all wholesale and most retail stores. The government also owns all state farms and controls other farms, called cooperatives, that are run by many people.

Since the revolutions of the late 1980s, many communist nations have abandoned that economic system. By the mid-1990s only Cuba and North Korea maintained a communist *economy*, although several other countries still operate under communist *governments*. In a communist economy, the people are not permitted to buy goods and to sell them at a profit or to employ others for any kind of profit-making venture.

Instead of letting the consumers decide what to buy, the government determines what goods are to be produced and what the cost of these goods will be. The items that the government considers essential are produced in larger quantities and are priced reasonably. Things such as good clothes, cars, or furniture, are priced very high. The production of these items is limited so that heavy machinery, industrial equipment, and military goods can be produced.

This government control over production is very inefficient. As the economy of a communist nation grows, it becomes more complicated. Government planning of every detail of economic activity becomes increasingly difficult.

The government also controlled wages. Because of this control, the people have little incentive to work hard and to do a good job. They realize that however hard they work, their wages will not increase until the government decides to raise them.

By free enterprise standards, economic freedom does not exist in communist nations. Individuals cannot start businesses that require labor other than their own. Individuals cannot own property that is productive. Workers cannot strike. Consumers are not able to indicate what goods they want produced.

The difference in atmosphere between communist countries and free enterprise countries is quickly noticeable. In communist countries little incentive for workers exists, and a sense of oppression and control by the government prevails. Because of this oppression, one of the foremost communist nations, the Soviet Union, split into smaller countries which want to try more capitalistic, free enterprise economic systems. Free enterprise gives many incentives to create good products when very little government control is involved with the production of goods. After living under Communism for many, many years, the people of the Soviet Union have seen the problems with government planning.

Complete the following statements.

2.34 The _____ system of the United States is called free enterprise.

2.35 The owners of business and industry in the free enterprise system are called

_____ .

2.36 In Communism, the _____ determines what goods will be produced and sets their prices.

Put an X beside the correct answers.

2.37 Which of the following are true about Communism?
   a. ☐   Production should belong to the people as a whole.
   b. ☐   The people can employ others to help make a profit.
   c. ☐   The consumers decide what to buy.
   d. ☐   Government owns all state farms.
   e. ☐   Government control over production is very efficient.
   f. ☐   The state owns all natural resources.

ROLE OF GOVERNMENT

The government, in the American economic system, plays three major roles. First, government has a regulatory function. This regulatory function means that government can intervene by making rules that will help the system to work more effectively. The types of rules it makes help to prevent fraud, to protect contracts, and to prevent **monopolies** and price fixing.

Second, the government collects taxes and spends them on public goods and services, such as schools, highways, and national defense. In the United States the people determine what resources ought to be used for the public. They make this determination through the people they elect to office. Most of the governmentally controlled services are things that the people believe cannot be effectively provided through private endeavor. These services include police and fire protection, postal service, schools, highways, Social Security, and unemployment payments.

Third, the government helps balance total supply and total demand. It does this function by increasing or decreasing its spending or by increasing or decreasing its taxes.

 Answer the following question.

2.38 What are the three major roles the government plays in the American economic system?

a. _____

b. _____

c. _____

MONEY

The growth of our economy and its stability are related to the amount of money spent and saved. When we think of money, we usually think of coins and bills. To an economist, however, money also means bank deposits—the demand deposits on which people write checks. In fact, bank deposits are the most important kind of money in the United States.

Money has three functions. First, money is a medium of exchange. Long ago people would trade or barter goods, in exchange for other goods. If one farmer had pigs but no dairy products, they would trade pigs for milk, cheese, or other products. As bartering became more and more complicated, the use of gold in exchange for products became more common. Eventually, coins and bills were developed so that people would not have to carry large amounts of gold. The gold was put into reserves where it remains to back up the coins and bills.

Second, money is a measure of value. Money helps us make comparisons of the value of various goods and services. If the price of one yo-yo is seventy-nine cents and the price of another is ninety-nine cents, and if they are made of the same materials and equal workmanship, the seventy-nine cent yo-yo is the better value. The amount of money needed to buy each one helps us to assess its value.

Third, money serves as a store of value. Money retains value and provides us with an easy way of saving because it is easily deposited in the bank.

 Answer the following questions.

2.39 What are money's three functions?

a. _____

b. _____

c. _____

2.40 To an economist, the word *money* means bank _____ as well as cash.

Created money. Money is something that can be created. Created money does not mean that a counterfeiter uses a printing press and goes to work. What created money does mean is that consumers borrow money from banks for goods and services that they want. If the bank decides to lend the money, it opens up an account against which the borrower can draw money from the bank. For example, a certain bank starts out with $1,000,000 in deposits from their customers. Someone comes to the bank to get a $25,000 loan to buy a house. The bank loans that money, using part of the $1,000,000. There is now $1,025,000 "being used" in the economy. One million still belongs to the original depositors, and the borrower now has $25,000 of the *created* money. A borrower can be a person, a businessperson, or even a government. Money can be borrowed from banks to buy such things as cars, new materials, new tools or machinery, or even defense equipment such as missiles, submarines, or airplanes.

Banks. The borrowing of money sounds easy, as though consumers could have everything they wanted just by asking the bank for the money. The amount of money that can be created is limited. The government controls this amount by requiring the banks to have reserves. If a bank were allowed to lend out as much money as it wanted to, soon it would have no gold to back up the currency. The money would lose its value and would become just paper. The reserves that the banks have are deposits in the Federal Reserve Bank and must not be less than a certain percentage of their demand deposits. A demand deposit is the type of deposit that a bank customer can ask to withdraw at any time. Once a bank lends out enough money to equal its percentage in the Federal Reserve Bank, it cannot lend any more. The size of the reserves is what determines the sum of money available for lending.

The functions of money in our economy are very important. Money is the basis for our entire system for production and consumption.

Write the letter for the correct answer on each line.

2.41 Created money means that consumers _____ .
a. deposit   b. borrow   c. withdraw

2.42 A deposit that can be withdrawn by the customer at any time is _____ .
a. interest   b. loan   c. a demand deposit

2.43 The sum of money available for lending by a bank is determined by _____ .
a. the size of the reserves   b. the government
c. the bank

TEACHER CHECK _____ _____
                                                 initials   date

Review the material in this section in preparation for the Self Test. This Self Test will check your mastery of this particular section as well as your knowledge of all previous sections.

SELF TEST 2

Complete these statements (each numbered item, 3 points).

2.01 In terms of wants and needs human _____ are limitless.

2.02 The economic system of the United States is called _____ .

2.03 Our wants have to be satisfied by the available _____ .

2.04 Saving means abstaining from _____ .

2.05 Economic rivalry among sellers for the consumers' dollars is called

_____ .

2.06 The economic system which is controlled and run by the government is called

_____ .

2.07 To an economist, _____ means bank deposits.

2.08 The amount of a bank's _____ determines how much it can lend.

Match these items (each answer, 2 points).

2.09	_____ profit	a. man-made resources used for production
2.010	_____ specialization	b. materials found in nature which man puts to his use
2.011	_____ consumers	c. reason that business people use their resources efficiently
2.012	_____ entrepreneur	
2.013	_____ demand	d. one person does a small portion of work on a larger project
2.014	_____ capital goods	
2.015	_____ factors of production	e. individuals, businesses, and different regions produce certain products
2.016	_____ human resources	f. people in society who are producers
2.017	_____ division of labor	g. people whose wants are being satisfied
2.018	_____ natural resources	h. available resources used for production
		i. another name for a businessman
		j. what determines how much is produced

Write the letter for the correct answer on each line (each answer, 2 points).

2.019 Minerals, trees, and animals are examples of _____ .
   a. human resources   b. capital goods   c. natural resources

2.020 Factories, buildings, and trucks are examples of _____ .
   a. natural resources   b. human resources   c. capital goods

2.021 Welders, assembly line workers, and printers are examples of _____ .
   a. natural resources   b. human resources   c. capital goods

2.022 Specialization makes regions more _____ .
   a. independent   b. interdependent   c. communistic

2.023 When the demand for a product is greater than the supply, prices and profits _____ .
   a. fall   b. remain the same   c. rise

2.024 One type of work that uses division of labor is _____ .
   a. automobile manufacture   b. gardening
   c. writing

2.025   The people that determine how much to produce are _____ .
   a. consumers   b. entrepreneurs   c. factory workers

2.026   Investment means spending on _____ .
   a. resources   b. capital goods   c. competition

2.027   The government spends our tax money on _____ .
   a. natural resources   b. market mechanism
   c. public goods and services

2.028   If competition is keen and prices are lowered, this market is called a _____ market.
   a. consumer's   b. producer's   c. stock

2.029   If consumers' wants are poorly satisfied and businesses are making large profits, this condi-

   tion is a _____ market.
   a. consumer's   b. producer's   c. stock

2.030   The development that has not taught us how to use natural resources wisely is the _____ .
   a. development of market mechanism

   b. development of synthetics

   c. development of science for agriculture

   d. development of machines for mass production

2.031   In the Communist system _____ .
   a. consumers decide what to buy

   b. private businesses own airlines and railroads

   c. people cannot strike

   d. there is economic freedom

2.032   The government does not provide _____ through taxes.
   a. police protection   b. Social Security   c. postal service   d. telephone service

2.033   God has promised to supply our _____ .
   a. needs   b. wants   c. available resources

Answer these questions (each numbered item, 5 points).

2.034   What are the three functions of money?

   a. _____

   b. _____

   c. _____

2.035 What are the three major roles that government plays in our economy?

a. _____

b. _____

c. _____

2.036 Put a C beside the statements that are true of communism, an F beside those that are true of free enterprise, and a B if it is true of both.

a. _____ laborers strike for better wages

b. _____ government has some effect on the economy

c. _____ producers set wages

d. _____ consumers decide what is produced

e. _____ natural resources are used in production

2.037 Put a C beside the statements that are true of communism, an F beside those that are true of free enterprise, and a B if it is true of both.

a. _____ unemployment exists

b. _____ entrepreneurs function quite freely

c. _____ government sets prices

d. _____ profit provides an incentive for work

e. _____ government owns the farms and mines

75 / 94   SCORE _____   TEACHER _____ _____
                                              initials   date

3. AN EXPERIMENT IN ECONOMY

To learn about different aspects of economics and how they relate to each other is important. To know the subject, you need to be able to apply what you have learned to your everyday life. This section should help you to do that.

SECTION OBJECTIVES

Review these objectives. When you have completed this section, you should be able to:

 2. Differentiate wants from needs.
 11. Develop a sound personal financial program.
 12. Make wiser choices as a consumer.
 13. Tell what the Bible says about money management.

BIBLICAL INSIGHTS

In attempting to make economics applicable to our lives, the best resource book we can use is the Bible. It has much to say about money and the way we should use it. For the believer, money's main purpose should be to provide his or her basic needs. As we saw earlier in Matthew 6:31 through 33, God promises to supply our needs. He also may supply many of our wants just because He loves us and likes to see us happy. Through the things God gives us, He is able to show us His power and His reality. He can give us things that we never dreamed were possible. In Philippians 4:19 the Bible says, "But my God shall supply all your needs according to His riches in glory by Christ Jesus." When we consider that God created this entire universe, we can realize how easily God can supply us with what we need.

God says in Proverbs 11:24, "There is that scattereth, and yet increaseth; and there is that witholdeth more than is meet, but it tendeth to poverty." These words warn us against being greedy. Sometimes this lesson is hard to apply to our lives. When we save some money, we like to hold onto it to buy something that we really want. If we follow what the Bible says, however, we should be willing to give it away if it will help someone in need. Of course, our attitude is also very important. If we give grudgingly or out of a sense of duty, we may as well not give at all, "...for God loveth a cheerful giver," (2 Corinthians 9:7).

The Bible also warns us against being too hasty. Proverbs 28:2 says, "He that hasteth to be rich hath an evil eye, and considereth not that poverty shall come upon him." The newspapers sometimes have stories of people who tried to get rich quickly. They are often in trouble because they cheated others, stole, lied, or covered up their illegal actions. In the end, they are usually sent to jail or fined heavily and are poorer than when they started.

God also has something to say about stubbornness in Proverbs 13:18: "Poverty and shame shall be to him that refuseth instruction: but he that regardeth reproof shall be honoured." Accepting criticism and making changes in our lives is difficult, but we can see that God will reward us if we do.

Laziness is something else that has to do with our economic success or failure. Proverbs 20:13 says, "Love not sleep, lest thou come to poverty, open thine eyes, and thou shalt be satisfied with bread." In Proverbs 6:11 we read, "So shall thy poverty come as one that travelleth, and thy want as an armed man." These harsh words should serve to remind us not to be lazy.

One other thing about which the Bible speaks quite clearly is debt. Proverbs 22:7 says, "The rich ruleth over the poor, and the borrower is servant to the lender." If money has been borrowed, an obligation exists to pay it back. Not doing so can cause hard feelings, put the borrower under pressure, and even cause legal action to be taken.

Some very expensive things such as houses and cars are difficult to pay for in cash, and their purchase may require borrowing money. Investigate the situation thoroughly, however, before making a commitment. Certainly you should decide whether the money is required for a need or merely for a want. Romans 13:8 clearly states, "Owe no man anything."

| Some purchases may require borrowing money.

Many other passages talk about prosperity, needs, sharing, and giving. In fact, the whole book of Proverbs is an excellent source of guidance in money matters.

Complete these statements.

3.1   Philippians 4:19 tells us that God will supply all our _____ .

3.2   The Bible encourages us to _____ freely to those in need.

Complete this activity.

3.3   List four things the Bible mentions that should be avoided in providing for ourselves.

   a. _____

   b. _____

   c. _____

   d. _____

PERSONAL FINANCIAL PROGRAM

In any financial program you need to set goals. Goals can be both long and short term. What these goals are, determines how your own program should be set up.

First of all, you will need to write down your economic goals. Do you need to start saving for college? Are you expected to buy your own clothes? Does your bike need repair? Are your shoes worn out? Do you want to go out for a soda with your friends this weekend? All of these things are goals. Some of them are immediate, some are a long way off. At this point in life, your parents probably supply—with the Lord's help—most of your needs. Although you are gaining more responsibility all the time, most of your goals will be more in the area of wants rather than in the area of needs. If your parents were making a budget, they would have to include things like house payments, car payments, doctor bills, food, clothing, entertainment for the family, vacation expenses, savings (either for something they want or for emergencies), gas and electric bills, gasoline, and maintenance for the car. Compared to their budget, yours will be simple. As you grow older you will need to change and to revise your budget. You will probably be earning more money in the future. Your needs will also change in the future.

Goals

Immediate	Intermediate	Long Range
soda after school 50¢	roller blades $50.00	savings for car $1,000
card for grandma $2.00	mountain bike $125.00	
lunch $2.50	gym shoes $75.00	
	Christmas gifts $25.00	

Steps to Setting Up a Financial Program

1. List your immediate, intermediate, and long-range goals. Think about them carefully, for they will be the basis for your budget.

2. Determine your available resources. Do you receive an allowance? Do you earn money by babysitting, cutting grass, delivering papers, shoveling walks, raking leaves, or pulling weeds? Any money that you receive is called income and should be listed.

3. If you are to follow Biblical principles about tithing, you should deduct a minimum of 10 percent of your income to give to the Lord's work. Tithe means one tenth and it is mentioned in the Bible (Leviticus 27:32) as the amount to give to the Lord. However, the New Testament only talks about giving without setting an amount. Ask the Lord what percentage He would have you give, but take that amount out first so that you will not find yourself caught short with nothing to give to the Lord. Remember, He is the one who gives us everything we have. Subtract the amount of your tithe from your available resources and you will have the amount that you have left to spend.

4. Next you must review your goals and determine your priorities to decide how much you want to allot for each one.

Goals		
Immediate (present)	**Intermediate (near future)**	**Long Range (future)**
Total income available:	$	
Deduct for tithe:	$	
Amount left to spend:	$	

For example, if you make $32.00 a week and are giving 10 percent tithe ($3.20), you will have $28.80 left to spend, to save, or to use as you see fit. You will probably want to spend some of the $28.80 on your immediate goals, some on your intermediate goals, and some on your long-range plans. The amount of money you receive each month should equal the amount you save and spend. Your long-range and intermediate goals will appear on your budget until they are reached. Instead of a weekly budget, you may want to make yours a monthly budget. You may want to model your budget after the one on the next page, or you may want to set up your own format.

Income		Weekly Savings and Expenses				
Source	**Amount**	**Item**	**Immediate**	**Intermediate**	**Long Range**	**$ Total**
Paper route	$20.00	Tithe	$3.20			**$3.20**
Allowance	$12.00	Savings			$2.00	**$2.00**
Mow lawns		Shoes		$1.50		**$1.50**
Baby sitting		Gifts		$0.50		**$0.50**
		Bike		$11.50		**$11.50**
		Skates		$11.25		**$11.25**
		Card	$2.00			**$2.00**
		Soda	$0.50			**$0.50**
		Socks	$2.00			**$2.00**
Totals	**$32.00**		**$7.70**	**$24.75**	**$2.00**	**$34.45**

In this case, the total of your wants comes to more than your available resources. Something must be changed to make the two totals come out even. You could forget your savings for a week. If you really want that car, however, you need to strive for your goal.

Now you have the choice of allotting less for your intermediate goals, delaying some of them, or doing without some of them. You may also choose to do without some of your immediate goals. Here are two alternatives:

Example 1						
Income		Weekly Savings and Expenses				
Source	**Amount**	**Item**	**Immediate**	**Intermediate**	**Long Range**	**$ Total**
Paper route	$20.00	Tithe	$3.20			**$3.20**
Allowance	$12.00	Savings			$10.00	**$10.00**
Mow lawns		Shoes		$10.00		**$10.00**
Baby sitting		Card	$1.50			**$1.50**
		Soda	$0.55			**$0.55**
		Socks	$5.50			**$5.50**
		Skates		$1.25		**$1.25**
Totals	**$32.00**		**$10.75**	**$11.25**	**$10.00**	**$32.00**

Example 2					
Income		**Weekly Savings and Expenses**			
Source	**Amount**	**Item**	**Immediate**	**Intermediate**	**Long Range**	**$ Total**
Paper route	$20.00	Tithe	$3.20			**$3.20**
Allowance	$12.00	Savings			$10.00	**$10.00**
Mow lawns		Shoes		$5.50		**$5.50**
Baby sitting		Gift		$1.50		**$1.50**
		Bike		$6.00		**$6.00**
		Skates		$5.25		**$5.25**
		Soda	$0.55			**$0.55**
Totals	**$32.00**		**$10.75**	**$11.25**	**$10.00**	**$32.00**

In each of these cases, you have met your goal of savings. However, you had to make choices about which items you wanted to be able to buy first. Try making up a budget of your own. You may want to include just one item for each kind of goal and work until that goal is reached. The important thing to do is to make sure that your income matches your expenses each week. The only sure way to do that is to write it down. If you follow this procedure, you can tell at a glance how much money you have. You should also keep a record of the money you have saved. The best way, of course, is to put the money in the bank where it will be earning interest. Putting it in the bank, also keeps you from "borrowing" from your own savings to buy things that were not in your budget, and makes you decide if what you want is really something you need. By keeping your budget, you will not be a person who has to borrow from others. You will have a sound economic program of your own.

Complete the following activities.

3.4 In any financial program you need to set _____ .

3.5 Referring to the "GOALS" illustration on page 37, list one item that would be considered an immediate want: _____ .

3.6 Leviticus 27:32 suggests _____ for tithe.

3.7 Three types of goals should be set for your budget. They are

a. _____ , b. _____ , and

c. _____ .

3.8 The important thing to remember in a budget is that your a. _____ should

always equal your b. _____ .

3.9 The best way to save money is to put it in a _____ .

TEACHER CHECK _____ _____
initials   date

3.10 Read Proverbs 31:10–27.

Write a 250-word paper discussing these verses in relation to what you have studied so far about economics in this LIFEPAC. If you are not sure how the two are related ask your teacher for help. Hand your paper in to your teacher.

TEACHER CHECK _____ _____
initials   date

Before you take this last Self Test, you may want to do one or more of these self checks.

1. _____ Read the objectives. See if you can do them.
2. _____ Restudy the material related to any objectives that you cannot do.
3. _____ Use the **SQ3R** study procedure to review the material:
   a. **S**can the sections.
   b. **Q**uestion yourself.
   c. **R**ead to answer your questions.
   d. **R**ecite the answers to yourself.
   e. **R**eview areas you did not understand.
4. _____ Review all vocabulary, activities, and Self Tests, writing a correct answer for every wrong answer.

SELF TEST 3

Complete these statements (each numbered item, 3 points).

3.01   Proverbs 20:13 says, "Love not sleep, lest thou come to _____ ."

3.02   Proverbs 11:24 says, "There is that _____ , and yet increaseth."

3.03   Proverbs 13:18: "Poverty and shame shall be to him that refuseth _____ ."

3.04   Philippians 4:19: "But my God shall supply all your _____ according to His riches in glory by Christ Jesus."

3.05   Proverbs 22:7: "... the borrower is _____ to the lender."

3.06   The suggested amount of tithe listed in the Bible is _____ percent.

3.07   In preparing a budget, the _____ must not exceed the income.

3.08   Competition is economic rivalry among sellers for the consumer's _____ .

3.09   If you are abstaining from consumption, you are _____ .

3.010   Consumers are people whose needs and _____ are satisfied.

3.011   Human resources are people in society who are _____ .

3.012   Besides cash, money also means bank _____ .

3.013   The auto industry uses the type of production called _____ production.

Answer true or false (each answer, 1 point).

3.014   _____   Romans 13:8 says, "Owe no man anything."

3.015   _____   God has promised to supply our wants.

3.016   _____   The economic system in which the government makes all the decisions is called free enterprise.

3.017   _____   God loves cheerful givers.

3.018   _____   Money's main purpose should be to supply our desires.

3.019   _____   Tithe literally means five percent.

3.020   _____   Consumers' wants will never be completely satisfied.

3.021   _____   Trying to get rich quickly is evil and leads to poverty.

3.022   _____   People who can accept criticism will end in poverty.

3.023   _____   If you work hard, you will have plenty to eat.

3.024   _____   Available resources are limitless.

3.025   _____   God often supplies some of our wants just because He loves us.

Write the letter for the correct answer on each line (each answer, 2 points).

3.026 If the demand for a good is large, the supply will _____ .
a. decrease   b. increase   c. remain the same

3.027 Every human being is a _____ .
a. business person   b. producer   c. consumer

3.028 In a consumer's market, prices tend to be _____ .
a. low   b. high

3.029 The government supplies, through taxes, _____ .
a. telephone service b. police protection c. banks

3.030 In a good budget, the first thing you should deduct for is _____ .
a. savings   b. candy   c. tithe

3.031 The New Testament tells us to _____ .
a. give our money   b. give 10 percent of our income
c. save our money

3.032 In Communist countries, the government controls _____ .
a. wages   b. capitalists   c. free enterprise

3.033 Available resources for a budget means _____ .
a. natural resources b. earned money   c. investments

3.034 Natural resources include _____ .
a. factories   b. buildings   c. minerals   d. trucks

3.035 A long-range goal would be considered a _____ .
a. college education b. baseball   c. concert ticket

3.036 Capital goods include _____ .
a. minerals   b. timber   c. animals   d. factories

3.037 In the free enterprise system _____ .
a. government controls wages
b. consumers decide what should be produced
c. there are no incentives for making good products

3.038 The three kinds of goals to set up a financial program include what? _____
a. immediate, inconsequential, and determined
b. inconsequential, intermediate, and mandatory
c. immediate, intermediate, and long range

3.039 The study of consumption, production, and distribution of wealth is called what? _____
a. Communism   b. economics   c. capitalism

3.040 Which of the following items represents a need? _____
    a. shelter   b. furniture   c. automobile

3.041 In working for economic success, Proverbs says we should avoid what? _____
    a. hard work   b. tithe   c. debt

3.042 The economic system where the government controls almost all economic activity is called _____ .
    a. free enterprise   b. Communism   c. liberalism

3.043 Human resources include what? _____
    a. trees and rivers   b. factories and trucks
    c. welders and managers   d. all of the above

3.044 Which of the following is *not* money? _____
    a. savings account   b. funds borrowed from a bank
    c. checking accounts   d. none of the above, they are all money

3.045 Business people produce goods primarily to make what? _____
    a. a name for themselves   b. a better nation
    c. a profit

3.046 A simple society is usually what? _____
    a. agrarian   b. Communist   c. consumer marketing

3.047 When one person does a small portion of work on a bigger project, what is this called? _____
    a. division of labor   b. consumer market   c. capital consumption

76 / 95   SCORE _____   TEACHER _____ _____
                                             initials   date

Before taking the LIFEPAC Test, you may want to do one or more of these self checks.

1. _____ Read the objectives. See if you can do them.
2. _____ Restudy the material related to any objectives that you cannot do.
3. _____ Use the **SQ3R** study procedure to review the material.
4. _____ Review activities, Self Tests, and LIFEPAC vocabulary words.
5. _____ Restudy areas of weakness indicated by the last Self Test.